VOLCANOES

Anita Ganeri

WAYLAND

First published in 2007 by Wayland

Copyright © Wayland 2007

Wayland,
Hachette Children's Books
338 Euston Road,
London NW1 3BH

Wayland Australia
Level 17/207 Kent Street
Sydney, NSW 2000

Editor: Susie Brooks
Managing Editor: Rasha Elsaeed
Designer: Tim Mayer, MayerMedia
Picture Researcher: Kathy Lockley

British Library Cataloguing in Publication Data
Ganeri, Anita, 1961-
    Volcanoes. - (Natural Disasters)
    1. Volcanoes - Juvenile literature
    I. Title
    551.2'1

ISBN 9780750249157

Wayland is a division of Hachette Children's Books, an
Hachette Livre UK company.

Photo credits: Cover, 8 ©Bettmann/Corbis; 1, 34-35 ©Andy
Johnstone/Panos Pictures; Bckgd 3-48 ©USGS/Ed Wolfe;
Bckgd (panels) 4-45 ©USGS/Dave Harlow; 4 ©Jim Sugar/
Corbis; 5 ©Karen Kasmauski/Corbis; 6 ©Charles O'Rear/
Corbis; 9 ©Sigurgeir Jonasson; Frank Lane Picture Agency/
Corbis; 10-11 ©Philppe Giraud/Goodlook/Corbis; 12, 13
©Corbis; 14-15 ©Philip Gould/Corbis, 16-17 ©USGS/Donald
A. Swanson; 18 ©USGS/Peter Lipman; 19 ©USGS/Austin
Post; 20, 21, 44 ©USGS/Lyn Topinka; 22-23 ©Carlos Angel/
Getty Images; 24-25, 26, 27 ©Jacques Langevin/Corbis
Sygma; 28-29 ©Nigel Dickenson/Still Pictures; 30 ©USGS/
John Ewert; 31 ©Albert Garcia/Corbis; 32 ©Rex Features/
Sipa Press; 33 ©Yann Arthus-Bertrand/Corbis; 36 ©Steve
Forrest/Insight/Panos Pictures; 37 ©Patrick Robert/Sygma
Corbis; 38-39 ©Michael Eudenbach/Getty Images; 41 ©AFP/
Getty Images; 42, 43 ©Reuters/Corbis; 45 ©Roger
Ressmeyer/Corbis

CONTENTS

What is a volcano?   4

Why volcanoes erupt   6

Volcano hazards   8

CASE STUDY: MOUNT PELÉE, MARTINIQUE, 1902   10

CASE STUDY: MOUNT ST HELENS, USA, 1980   16

CASE STUDY: NEVADO DEL RUIZ, COLOMBIA, 1985   22

CASE STUDY: MOUNT PINATUBO, PHILIPPINES, 1991   28

CASE STUDY: SOUFRIERE HILLS, MONTSERRAT,
SINCE 1995   34

CASE STUDY: NYIRAGONGO, DEMOCRATIC REPUBLIC
OF CONGO, 2002   40

Eruption prediction and protection   44

Glossary   46

Further Information   47

Index   48

What is a volcano?

This volcano is blasting molten rock from the ground, producing a firey lava fountain and lava flow.

Many people think of a volcano as being a cone-shaped mountain with red-hot lava (molten rock) flowing from the top. This sort of mountain is a volcano, but to a volcanologist (a scientist who studies volcanoes) a volcano is simply a place where molten rock, ash and gas emerge from inside the Earth. Many volcanoes are cone-shaped, but others are just cracks in the ground. Many volcanoes do spew out streams of lava, but others explode violently instead. Flowing lava, explosions of ash and other volcanic effects have caused some of the world's worst natural disasters.

A volcanic eruption

When a volcano throws out material from within, it is erupting. The ways in which volcanoes erupt can vary widely. When some volcanoes erupt, they produce rivers of molten lava. When others erupt, they produce vast clouds of ash, and little or no lava. Some volcanoes produce a mixture of both lava flows and ash. All eruptions also produce gases.

Volcanic eruptions are extremely hazardous events. Anybody and anything near an erupting volcano faces serious dangers, such as being burnt by scalding lava, choked by clouds of ash and gas or hit by lumps of flying rock. Erupting volcanoes also set off secondary hazards, such as fires, mudflows, landslides and tsunamis (giant waves at sea).

Volcanoes and the landscape

Over hundreds, thousands or millions of years, volcanoes build up and alter the landscape. Lava cools and turns solid, and ash builds up in layers, creating new rocks on the surface. This new rock forms cone-shaped mountains and even whole mountain ranges. Volcanoes that erupt under the sea build up islands and chains of islands.

Living with volcanoes

Even though volcanoes are so dangerous, hundreds of millions of people around the world live close to them and some large cities are located in danger areas. Why do so many people live near volcanoes? One of the main reasons is that the soil around volcanoes is very rich and good for agriculture. Another is that shortage of space means that many people have no choice over where they live. And many cities were founded before people understood the real dangers of volcanoes.

Japanese farmers work in fields of volcanic soil close to the dormant Mount Fuji.

ACTIVE, DORMANT, EXTINCT

Volcanologists categorize volcanoes as active, dormant or extinct. An active volcano is one that is erupting today or that we know has erupted in the last 10,000 years. A dormant volcano is an active volcano that is not erupting at the moment. An extinct volcano is a dead volcano that experts believe will never erupt again.

Why volcanoes erupt

Volcanoes occur where molten rock from many kilometres under the Earth's surface forces its way out above the ground. When it is underground, the molten rock is known as magma. It is lighter in weight than the rock around it, so it pushes up through the surrounding rock, like a beach ball floating up through water, finding the easiest route to the surface. When the magma reaches the surface, it either flows out as lava or breaks up and cools to form ash and small pieces of solid rock.

Under the surface

Volcanoes form only in certain parts of the world. In many places there are no volcanoes at all. To understand why, it is important to know about the internal structure of the Earth. Earth has three layers – the central core, a very thick layer called the mantle, and a much thinner surface, or crust. The crust is between 5 and 100 kilometres thick. The crust and the topmost part of the mantle make up a layer known as the lithosphere. This layer is broken up into about 30 giant pieces, known as tectonic plates. A layer of softer rock beneath the lithosphere allows the plates to move about very slowly.

This island volcano, called Anak Krakatau, emerged after an eruption in 1927. It lies over a subduction zone in Indonesia. An older volcano, Krakatau, exploded here in 1883.

Plate boundaries

The places where tectonic plates touch each other are known as plate boundaries, and these are where most volcanoes happen. Divergent boundaries are places where two plates move away from each other, leaving a gap. Here magma rises to fill the gap, forming volcanoes. Convergent boundaries, also called subduction zones, are places where two plates move towards each other. When they collide, one of the plates dips down beneath the other. As its rocks are pushed into the mantle, they melt, forming magma. The magma pushes up through the uppermost plate and volcanoes are formed.

Magma ingredients

Magma is a mixture of minerals and gases such as water vapour and carbon dioxide. There are different types of magma, with different mixtures of minerals and gases. The magma that emerges at divergent boundaries is normally runny. As it reaches the surface, the gas it contains escapes easily and the minerals form lava flows. The magma that emerges at convergent boundaries is much thicker. Its gas cannot escape so easily and it causes explosive eruptions that produce clouds of ash and rock. These are the most dangerous volcanic events.

The purple spots on this map are areas of volcanic activity. The black lines represent the tectonic plate boundaries, and the arrows show the plates' direction of movement.

VOLCANO TYPES

Volcanologists classify volcanoes by their shape and the materials they are made from. A shield volcano is made of layers of solidified lava. It has gently sloping sides. A composite cone, or stratovolcano, is steep-sided and made up of layers of solidified lava and ash. The opening in any volcano, through which it erupts, is called the vent.

Volcano hazards

MUDFLOWS

Volcanic mudflows, called lahars, happen when water mixes with volcanic ash. The water often comes from snow and ice melted by the heat of an eruption. Mudflows travel fast, and when they stop they set hard, like concrete.

A volcanic eruption creates many different hazards, from red-hot lava flows to deadly tsunami waves at sea. Some of these hazards affect only the area local to a volcano, but others cause damage hundreds of kilometres away. When the largest volcanoes, called 'supervolcanoes', erupt they can affect the whole planet.

Lava flows

When lava erupts from a volcano it pours down the mountain's sides until it cools and solidifies. The flow can travel tens of kilometres from the volcano itself. Lava is often thrown into the air as it leaves a volcano's vent, forming lava fountains. Because of its intense heat, lava destroys everything in its path. However, it rarely kills people because lava normally flows at less than 10 kph.

Pyroclasts

A pyroclast is a piece of rock that is thrust into the air by a volcanic eruption. Pyroclasts are thrown upwards by gas released from magma as it reaches the surface. There are several different kinds of pyroclast. Ash is made up of tiny particles of rock. It is formed when frothy magma blows apart and the pieces cool quickly in the air. Pumice is made up of grape-sized pieces of solidified lava, full of gas pockets. The largest pyroclasts are known as volcanic bombs. These are fist-sized or larger. Some land before they completely solidify and then break open, releasing lava. Volcanic bombs are a hazard within a few kilometres of an erupting volcano.

These homes in Iceland are under threat from lava flows pouring from the erupting Heimaey volcano in the background.

Ash clouds

Thick, gas-filled lava breaks up into ash as it leaves a volcano's vent. The gas blasts the ash upwards, forming a tall cloud called an eruption column. The heat of the gas carries the ash further upwards, and eruption columns often reach over 15 kilometres in height. Ash can be carried for thousands of kilometres through the atmosphere. It blocks sunlight and causes temperatures to fall. Where the ash falls back to the ground, it smothers everything, killing plants and crops, damaging machinery and buildings and making it difficult for people and animals to breathe.

Ash avalanches

Ash clouds are often so heavy with pyroclasts that they cannot keep rising upwards. Instead they collapse, forming avalanches of ash and gas that stream down the sides of volcanoes. These avalanches are called pyroclastic flows. They move at speeds of up to 160 kph, and inside the flow the temperature can reach 600°C. A pyroclastic flow destroys everything it touches. Anybody caught in a pyroclastic flow stands no chance of survival.

MOUNT PELÉE, MARTINIQUE, 1902

St Pierre is a city on the coast of the Caribbean island of Martinique. In 1902, St Pierre was Martinique's main city, with a population of 20,000 people. It had picturesque buildings and streets and a thriving tourist industry. Rising behind St Pierre, just 7 kilometres away, is Mount Pelée, a 1,397-metre high active stratovolcano. Mount Pelée erupted in 1902. The eruption completely destroyed St Pierre and killed all of its inhabitants. It was the most deadly volcanic disaster of the twentieth century.

VOLCANIC ISLANDS

Martinique is one of a chain of islands in the West Indies. It is about 60 kilometres long and about 20 kilometres wide. The islands of the West Indies lie along the edge of the Caribbean tectonic plate and were all formed by volcanic activity. Some of the volcanoes are extinct while others, including Mount Pelée, are active.

The volcano stirs

There were several months of volcanic activity at Mount Pelée in 1902, before the main eruption. Volcanic gases spewed out in January. In April there were small explosions from the summit, minor earthquakes, and ash and cinders fell on St Pierre. On 27 April the summit crater began to fill with water from inside the volcano. In early May, explosions created an eruption column and ash fell around the volcano. On 5 May, the crater rim collapsed and boiling water streamed down the volcano's slopes. The water mixed with old layers of ash, forming a mudflow that poured into the local river, killing 23 workers at a distillery.

Local concern

Naturally the people of St Pierre were worried by the earthquakes, ash, gas and mudflows. They were aware of some of the other dangers of volcanoes, such as lava flows. Would these be the next hazard from Mount Pelée? Some residents moved out to the island's second city, Fort-de-France, which lay a safe distance from the volcano. Others fled the island altogether on steamships. But most people stayed in St Pierre.

Persuaded to stay

There were two reasons why people stayed. Firstly, local officials visited the volcano on 5 May and reported that the volcanic activity was not serious enough for people to evacuate. Their report appeared in the local newspaper, *Les Colonies*, and people were reassured. Secondly, an election was due on 11 May. The governor needed people's votes to stay in power, and he persuaded the editor of *Les Colonies* to play down the danger. He also ordered troops to stop people leaving for Fort-de-France. In fact, the population of St Pierre actually grew to about 28,000 as people arrived from the countryside because they thought the city would be safer.

This photograph shows Mount Pelée as it stands today. All the houses in the foreground would be in danger from pyroclastic flows if the volcano erupted again.

MOUNT PELÉE, MARTINIQUE, 1902

ERUPTION COSTS

- 2 towns (St Pierre and Morne Rouge) destroyed
- 28,000 deaths in St Pierre
- 1,500 deaths in Morne Rouge
- 20 ships lost in St Pierre harbour

Mount Pelée erupts

On 6 May 1902, new magma rose into Mount Pelée. A dome of lava grew in the crater, and the eruption column shot higher. Then, in the morning of 8 May, a colossal explosion ripped through the side of the volcano, releasing a mixture of searing hot gas, ash and lumps of rock. Some of the blast was directed upwards, forming a new eruption column, and some was directed sideways. The sideways blast started a pyroclastic flow that travelled down the volcano's slopes towards the sea. Hugging the ground, and travelling at more than 150 kph, the flow reached St Pierre, 7 kilometres away, in under a minute.

Effects of the eruption

The buildings of St Pierre could not withstand the immense pressure from the pyroclastic flow, and all were destroyed. Walls a metre thick were flattened and a 3-tonne statue was picked up and hurled along. The flow swept out into the harbour where more than 20 ships were capsized and set on fire. Temperatures of up to 1,000°C started blazes in the town, which were made even worse as thousands of barrels of flammable rum exploded.

The inhabitants of St Pierre had no warning and stood no chance. They were killed by the force of the blast and by breathing hot ash and gas. Out of 28,000 people in the city, there were just two survivors. The city burned for several days, and on 20 May another pyroclastic flow destroyed anything that was left.

Clouds of choking ash rise from the pyroclastic flows as Mount Pelée erupts.

Survivors clamber through the ruins of St Pierre. The city's vibrant streets were reduced to little more than rubble and ash.

The survivors

One of the city's only two survivors was a 27-year-old labourer called Ludger Sylbaris (also known as Louis-Auguste Cyparis). He had been imprisoned in the city's dungeon, which had only a small opening to the outside air. Sylbaris was hit by a blast of hot gas and ash. His legs, arms and back were badly burned but he survived by holding his breath. He was rescued four days after the eruption. The other survivor was Léon Compere-Léandre, a shoemaker. He was sitting on his doorstep in the street when the flow struck. He struggled indoors, feeling his arms and legs burning. After falling unconscious for an hour, he made his way to safety.

EYEWITNESS

❝ Before I got to the cave, I looked back. The whole of the side of the mountain seemed to open up and boil down on the screaming people. I was burned a good deal by the stones and ashes that came flying about the boat. ❞

Havivra Da Ifrile, a young girl who was on the outskirts of the city, on the lower slopes of the volcano, when the pyroclastic flow began. She ran to the shore, jumped into a boat and rowed to a local cave.

MOUNT PELÉE, MARTINIQUE, 1902

A lack of knowledge

Thousands of lives could have been saved if St Pierre had been evacuated when Mount Pelée began to erupt in early May. But local officials did not know about the threat of pyroclastic flows. The scientist who had helped them to prepare the report on the dangers of Mount Pelée was not a volcano expert but a schoolteacher. In any case, in 1902 not even volcano experts knew that pyroclastic flows existed. They thought the only threat was from lava flows, and a river valley protected St Pierre from these. Today's volcanologists would have known that pyroclastic flows were likely during an eruption of Mount Pelée.

A new hazard

Scientists studied the eruption of Mount Pelée and its effects on St Pierre closely. This taught them new things about eruptions of stratovolcanoes and especially about pyroclastic flows and how they move. At the time, Martinique was a French colony and French volcanologists called these devastating flows *nuées ardentes*, which means 'glowing clouds'. This name comes from the fact that a pyroclastic flow glows red from the intense heat inside.

News of the eruption spread quickly around the world, and scientists studying other volcanoes became aware of the dangers of pyroclastic flows. A volcano observatory (the second ever to be built in the world) was set up to monitor Mount Pelée and was operated until 1925. There was a another eruption between 1929 and 1932, which produced more pyroclastic flows but little damage.

ANIMAL ACTIVITY

Pyroclastic flows were not the only hazard of Mount Pelée. Earthquakes and volcanic gases drove insects and snakes from the volcano's slopes. Red ants, giant centipedes and poisonous snakes bit farm animals and people. About 50 people and 200 animals died from these bites.

Mount Pelée today

Some parts of St Pierre were rebuilt, but most remain in ruins. Today St Pierre is a village with just a few thousand inhabitants. Martinique's main city is now Fort-de-France in the south of the island, far from the volcano. However, thousands of people still live in towns and villages around Mount Pelée. There have been no eruptions since 1932, but the volcano is still active and it could erupt again at any time. There is a new observatory, run by the French government, on a hill 8 kilometres south of Mount Pelée. Volcanologists there receive data from instruments that detect volcanic gases, earthquakes and ground movements. This will enable them to give plenty of warning of future eruptions and hopefully save thousands of lives.

In St Pierre today, people live in new housing built alongside ruins from the 1902 eruption. Visitors to Martinique can see the crumbling remains of the once grand city centre.

MOUNT ST HELENS, USA, 1980

Mount St Helens is a volcano in the state of Washington, USA. During an eruption in 1980, Mount St Helens exploded, sending a sideways blast across the landscape. The eruption was being monitored by volcanologists but the explosion was far more violent than expected. It killed 57 people, many of whom were within areas that experts thought were safe. Studying this disaster has taught volcanologists a great deal about this sort of explosive eruption.

PREVIOUS ERUPTIONS

Mount St Helens had erupted many times before 1980. The oldest ash deposits found in the area are 40,000 years old. The previous eruption lasted from 1800 until the 1850s. It was seen by local Native Americans and settlers. The Native Americans called the volcano Louwala-Clough, which means 'smoking mountain'.

This is Mount St Helens as it looked on 27 March 1980, about seven weeks before the main eruption when this side of the mountain collapsed. Steam and ash are erupting from the summit crater.

Mount St Helens country

Mount St Helens is one of many volcanoes in the Cascade Range of mountains. They are all stratovolcanoes that have formed over a subduction zone, where the Pacific tectonic plate dips below the North American plate. Before the 1980 eruption, Mount St Helens was an almost perfect cone shape and was known as the 'Fujiyama of America', after the similarly shaped Mount Fuji in Japan. It stood 2,950 metres high and was usually capped with snow. Mount St Helens lies in a wilderness area, surrounded by hills covered with coniferous forests. There are several lakes close by.

Spirit Lake is located 6 kilometres from the volcano's peak. Before the eruption, this was an attractive recreational area, popular with fishermen, hunters, walkers, climbers and campers. There were holiday lodges around the shore of Spirit Lake and tourism provided an important income for the local people. Forestry companies owned much of the land and there were logging camps scattered around the area.

St Helens wakes

The first sign that Mount St Helens was coming to life in early 1980 was a small earthquake that shook the ground on 20 March. More earthquakes followed. Over the next two months, more than 10,000 small earthquakes were recorded in the region. They showed that magma was moving up into the volcano. There were also eruptions of steam and gas. As April passed, the north side of the mountain began to bulge outwards and upwards. By the middle of May, the bulge was 80 metres high. The magma was building up pressure underneath.

DISASTER DAYS

20 MARCH 1980
Small earthquakes show that Mount St Helens is coming to life.

22 MARCH
Earthquakes under the volcano increase in strength and the mountain slopes are closed to visitors.

27 MARCH
Small eruptions of steam rise from the crater. An exclusion zone is set up around the volcano.

APRIL-MAY
Bulge grows on the volcano's north flank.

1 MAY
Road blocks are set up by the National Guard.

18 MAY
8.32 am North side of the mountain collapses.

8.33 am Giant pyroclastic flows move over ridges to the north of the volcano.

10 am Ash begins to fall on the city of Yakima, 150 kilometres away.

1980-1986
A series of minor eruptions builds a dome nearly 300 metres high in the gaping crater left by the 1980 eruption.

1982
Mount St Helens National Volcano Monument is created.

MOUNT ST HELENS, USA, 1980

News that Mount St Helens was stirring spread quickly. It was to be the first eruption on the US mainland since 1914, and everybody wanted to see it for themselves. The volcano soon became a media and tourist hotspot. Television crews, reporters and photographers arrived, along with thousands of sightseers. The main road into the area became clogged with traffic. Locals set up stalls selling souvenirs and fast food. Every day, dozens of light aircraft and helicopters buzzed around the volcano, causing several collisions. Some helicopters even landed on the crater rim.

The bulge that grew on the north side of the volcano is clear to the left of this picture. It grew at up to 1.5 metres per day. The volcanologist in the foreground is measuring its height.

Warnings and evacuations

Volcanologists from the US Geological Survey arrived at Mount St Helens in the days after the first earthquakes. They set up a network of scientific instruments, such as seismometers and tiltmeters, to monitor the progress of the eruption. They realized that an explosive eruption was probably soon to come and informed local officials. The emergency services responded by setting up an exclusion zone around the volcano with road blocks to prevent people from entering. They also asked people inside the zone, such as forestry workers and lodge owners, to evacuate for their own safety.

Local resentment

Many locals, reporters, sightseers and forestry workers resented being told to stay away from the volcano. For some, the evacuation was costing them money. They angrily told officials that they had a right to go wherever they wanted, and that the setting up of an exclusion zone was an over reaction. Many people broke down the road-block barriers or drove around them. In the end, local officials called in the National Guard to operate the road blocks. As the bulge on the mountainside grew ominously larger, the exclusion zone was expanded.

The eruption

By mid-May, the bulge on the north side of Mount St Helens had grown so large it was unstable. On the morning of 18 May, an earthquake under the volcano caused the whole north face of the mountain to collapse. It was the largest landslide in recorded history. The collapse released the pressure on the magma inside, which exploded as the gas in it expanded. A pyroclastic flow blasted across the landscape, racing over ridges 300 metres high. It travelled 30 kilometres before it stopped, and devastated 650 square kilometres of forests and lakes. Another blast went upwards, forming an eruption column 19 kilometres high. More than 300 metres of rock were blown off the top of the volcano.

This aerial photograph shows Mount St Helens from the south on the day it erupted. The opposite side of the mountain was blasted away.

UNEXPECTED VIOLENCE

The power of the explosion was much greater than the volcanologists had expected. They had only limited knowledge of the eruptions of stratovolcanoes and had based their predictions on their experience of eruptions in Hawaii, where the volcanoes do not erupt explosively.

MOUNT ST HELENS, USA, 1980

ERUPTION COSTS

- 57 deaths
- 650 square kilometres of land devastated
- 57,000 square kilometres affected by ash fall
- Millions of forestry trees destroyed
- Estimated repair bill: US$1.1 billion

Eruption effects

The landslide on the north face of the mountain buried the countryside around Spirit Lake under tens of metres of debris, which lay in great heaps. The pyroclastic flow knocked flat millions of trees and turned the landscape into an ash-covered wasteland. The heat inside the flow was so great that it melted the plastic parts of cars that were caught in it. Water released from the volcano's rocks, from melting snow and from the local rivers mixed with debris and ash, forming mudflows. These rushed down the river valleys and drained into the Columbia River to the south. The mudflows wrecked bridges and buildings along the rivers.

Despite precautions, 57 people died in the 1980 eruption. They included sightseers, forestry workers, campers and volcanologists. Some had been inside the exclusion zone, but most were outside where they thought they would be safe. Victims were killed by the heat and ash of the pyroclastic flow, by falling trees and by the mudflows.

Fawn Lake is about 15 kilometres north of Mount St Helens, which you can see in the distance in this photograph. Most of the trees in the area were flattened by the blast.

A helicopter lands on the ash-covered landscape near Mount St Helens, three months after the eruption.

Millions of tonnes of ash were carried into the atmosphere by the eruption column. The ash fell over a wide area, extending hundreds of kilometres from Mount St Helens. Some places received several centimetres of ash. The ash layer caused the closure of roads and airports, damaged power supplies and took many days to clear up.

A new monument

Forestry workers cleared away hundreds of thousands of trees that had been felled by the eruption, so that their wood was not wasted, and planted new ones in their place. Rivers were dredged to remove the ash left by the mudflows. Army engineers built a drainage tunnel from Spirit Lake in case the lake overflowed and caused another mudflow.

The authorities decided to leave the area around Mount St Helens as it was, to allow it to recover naturally. In 1982 they created the Mount St Helens National Volcano Monument and built visitor centres and observation stations. People visit the area to learn about volcanoes and to walk and climb. Scientists visit Mount St Helens to study how plants and animals are establishing themselves again.

CASCADES OBSERVATORY

The Cascades Volcano Observatory was set up in the town of Vancouver, near Mount St Helens, soon after the eruption. It is run by the US Geological Survey, and monitors Mount St Helens and other Cascade Range volcanoes so that warnings can be given if major eruptions are likely in the future.

NEVADO DEL RUIZ, COLOMBIA, 1985

Nevado del Ruiz is a volcano in Colombia, South America. In 1985, a small eruption of Nevado del Ruiz triggered massive mudflows that swept down the volcano's slopes and into river valleys. Communities along the rivers were destroyed, including the town of Armero, which was completely wiped out along with 22,000 of its inhabitants. Volcanologists predicted the eruption, but poor emergency planning and communications meant that there were no evacuations. This event was the worst volcanic disaster since the destruction of St Pierre more than 80 years earlier (see pages 10-15).

PREVIOUS MUDFLOWS

We know about two other eruptions of Nevado del Ruiz in the past – in 1585 and in 1845. Both caused mudflows in the river valleys. The 1845 eruption killed more than 1,000 people, many along the Rio Lagunillas. But people gradually forgot this disaster, and 50 years later the town of Armero began to grow on top of the old, dried-out mudflows.

Rivers and towns

Nevado del Ruiz is one of a line of stratovolcanoes at the northern end of the Andes mountain range. The volcanoes are in a subduction zone where the Nazca tectonic plate slides under the South American plate. Nevado del Ruiz is 5,400 metres high and has a permanent cap of snow and ice. Steep-sided river valleys carry water drained from its slopes.

The town of Armero lay on a flat plain, about 75 kilometres east of the volcano's summit. It was located next to the Rio Lagunillas, a river that emerged from the Lagunillas Canyon a few kilometres upstream. The city was a thriving centre for rice and cotton production, with a population of about 23,000 people.

This photograph shows the snow-capped summit of Nevado del Ruiz, with steam erupting from the vent.

First warnings

The first signs that Nevado del Ruiz might erupt anew were several earthquakes and fountains of steam late in 1984. These continued throughout 1985 and gradually increased in power. In September 1985, scientists from the Colombian Institute of Geology and Mining, together with international experts, surveyed the volcano and set up instruments to monitor the eruption. In October they completed a hazard map that showed the areas at risk from mudflows if the eruption worsened. Armero would be hit. An emergency committee was formed. The scientists advised government officials and local authorities about the dangers of mudflows.

ACTION ALERT

The Civil Defence organization prepared for an eruption by gathering together emergency equipment, improving radio communications, talking to the public about the risks, and distributing advice leaflets.

NEVADO DEL RUIZ, COLOMBIA, 1985

A failure of communications

At an emergency meeting on 13 November, scientists, local officials and Red Cross officers discussed how they would respond if the eruption got worse. That same afternoon things began to deteriorate. Ash and small chunks of rock began to fall on Armero. The police in Armero and other communities were warned, but no evacuation was ordered. In fact, during the day, local radio stations told people that there was little danger and to stay at home. The local officials did not want people to panic and they were reluctant to evacuate anyone if it was not necessary.

A mud-covered plain lies where Armero once stood. Beyond it is the Lagunillas Canyon, where the mudflow emerged.

EYEWITNESS

The mud was coming behind us. We had run two blocks, but by the third block, we were surrounded.

Edgar Hernandez, aged 19. He and his brother were two of the lucky survivors in Armero. They became trapped on a patch of high ground with dozens of other people. They were rescued the next day, but lost many members of their family.

ERUPTION COSTS

- Armero destroyed; other towns damaged
- Armero abandoned
- 23,000 deaths in Armero
- 1,800 deaths in Chinchina

The eruption and mudflow

In the evening of 13 November, the main eruption began. Four pyroclastic flows moved across the mountaintop. Their heat melted snow and ice, releasing huge amounts of water, which mixed with ash and flowed down into the river valleys. As the mudflows travelled they were swelled by river water and more falling debris. Some flows became 50 metres deep. Moving at up to 40 kph, they swept more than 100 kilometres from the volcano. Two hours after the eruption a mudflow poured from the end of the Lagunillas Canyon into Armero. The flow was equivalent to ten Olympic-sized swimming pools of mud every second. It spread out on to the plains, becoming 2.5 kilometres wide in places.

Mudflow effects

Darkness and bad weather meant that by the time the scientists monitoring Nevado del Ruiz realized what was happening, the mud was well on its way to Armero. The scientists raised the alarm as soon as they could. Warnings were broadcast on official radio channels, but few people were listening. Most people were in bed when the lahar hit the town.

As the sticky mud poured into the streets, it was up to 6 metres deep. It flowed through some buildings, knocked down others, crushed cars and carried away the debris. As the hours passed, more waves of mud arrived. When the mud eventually stopped flowing it became almost solid, trapping everything in it.

The first the sleeping inhabitants of Armero knew about the lahar was a rumbling noise and shouting in the streets. The town's lights failed. Some people managed to run to high ground, but most were caught by the mud. Only 2,000 (fewer than one in ten) residents survived. Another 1,800 were killed by mudflows in the town of Chinchina on the western side of the mountain. Thousands more were injured.

NEVADO DEL RUIZ, COLOMBIA, 1985

Rescue workers carefully pull lucky survivors from the thick, sticky mud. Dozens of people were saved in this way, while thousands more died in the ruins of their homes.

Rescue at Armero

News of the disaster in Armero was spread by radio operators. Members of the Civil Defence and Red Cross went to the scene but had to wait until it was light before they could organize a rescue. Rescuers pulled survivors from the setting mud, standing on debris to keep themselves from falling in. The mud made road travel difficult, and at first only a few helicopters were available to transport survivors to hospital. The search for survivors went on for several days over the wide area affected. Refugee camps and field hospitals were set up in neighbouring towns. Some people simply set off on foot to other, safer communities, hoping they could stay with family and friends.

Armero abandoned

People returned to Armero to salvage what they could and to try to find missing friends and relatives, but they did not stay. The town of Armero was never rebuilt. Its remains are still hidden under the solidified mud that destroyed it in 1985. The area has been officially declared a cemetery as thousands of people's bodies remain buried under the mud. The survivors lost everything. Many spent months in temporary accommodation in local refugee centres. Some rented homes in nearby towns, and some moved into housing built for them by the Colombian government. Businesses lost in Armero, such as agricultural supply companies, reopened in other places.

Lessons from Armero

The loss of Armero and its inhabitants was a natural disaster that could have been avoided. Scientists had predicted the mudflows and the Civil Defence had told people of the dangers, but the townspeople were not evacuated. Was anybody in particular to blame? The answer is probably no. The disaster was caused by poor planning, human error and an overall lack of experience.

The scientists from the Colombian Institute of Geology and Mining and international experts had monitored the volcano, drawn up hazard maps and made local officials aware of the risks. But they had not been able to predict exactly when or where the flows would strike. Darkness and poor weather had delayed their final warnings.

The Civil Defence had also recognized the hazards of Nevado del Ruiz. They had given out information about eruptions to the public, but they had not stressed the potential dangers of mudflows.

Local authorities and government officials had never really believed that Armero was at risk. They had been reluctant to call for an evacuation without reliable information from the scientists.

The residents of Armero were also unprepared. They had been given hazard maps and information about eruptions, but few had believed they were in danger, especially as local radio stations had said that a serious eruption was unlikely.

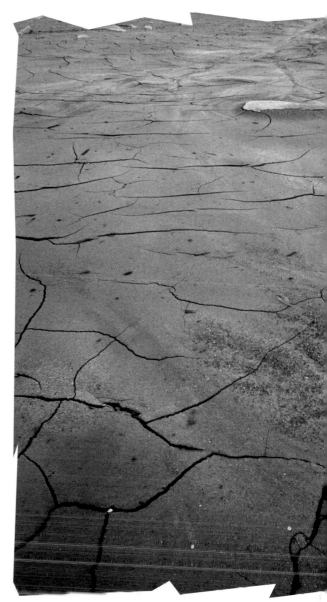

As the mud covering Armero slowly dried out, it became hard and cracked. It would have been impossible to dig the town out again.

NEVADO DEL RUIZ TODAY

Nevado del Ruiz is still an active volcano and it could easily set off mudflows in the future. More than 50,000 people live in the danger area, some in cities larger than Armero. The volcano is now closely monitored, better emergency plans are in place and the public is better informed. Next time there is an eruption, a disaster should be avoided.

MOUNT PINATUBO, PHILIPPINES, 1991

In 1991, a volcano in the Philippines called Mount Pinatubo experienced the most explosive volcanic eruption of the twentieth century. Pinatubo's eruption was a big surprise, even to volcanologists, as the mountain had been dormant for about 600 years. People were killed by mudflows and pyroclastic flows, but tens of thousands of lives were saved because volcanologists accurately predicted the explosive phase of the eruption and evacuations were carried out.

The geography of Pinatubo

Mount Pinatubo is a stratovolcano that was formed over a subduction zone where the Philippine tectonic plate meets the Eurasian plate. The volcano now stands 1,445 metres high, and is 40 kilometres wide at its base. It is part of the island of Luzon in the north of the Philippines, and is one of a north-south line of active volcanoes on the island. Before the 1991 eruption, the upper slopes of Mount Pinatubo were covered with dense forests.

Pinatubo is 55 kilometres north of Manila, a city of 10 million people. To the volcano's east are wide plains covered with fertile volcanic soil, where the main crop is rice. This is the Philippines' most productive agricultural area. There is additional farmland to the west, between the mountain range and the sea. Many communities also farm alongside the rivers that drain the volcano's slopes.

EVIDENCE OF PAST ERUPTIONS

In 1991, scientists surveyed the area around Mount Pinatubo. They found deep deposits of ash, left by previous eruptions, up to 20 kilometres from the summit. This told them that Pinatubo had erupted violently in the past, so they prepared for similar events again. They drew up hazard maps to show the potential danger areas, which included their own base.

This photograph was taken before Mount Pinatubo erupted in 1991. After the eruption the forests seen here were ruined.

Monitoring an eruption

The 1991 eruption began on 2 April with small explosions of steam from vents on the volcano's upper slopes. Villagers reported these to the authorities. Scientists at the Philippine Institute of Volcanology and Seismology (PHIVOLCS) responded when they heard the news. They put seismometers on the volcano and were alarmed when their instruments detected hundreds of small earthquakes deep under the ground. Magma was on the move.

The scientists ordered immediate evacuations of villages within 10 kilometres of the summit. They also called in a team of volcanologists from the US Geological Survey. Together, the international team put in place a network of seismometers, tiltmeters and gas analysis instruments. They set up an observation post at the Clark Air Base at the eastern edge of the volcano and monitored earthquakes, ground movements and gases coming from the vents. They used computers to draw three-dimensional models of the volcano, which showed clearly the progress of the eruption.

DISASTER DAYS

2 APRIL 1991
Small eruptions of steam show that Mount Pinatubo is coming to life.

5 APRIL
Volcanologists install their first seismometer on the summit.

LATE APRIL
Pinatubo Volcano Observatory is built.

MID-LATE MAY
Emissions of sulphur dioxide increase.

9 JUNE
Volcanologists raise the alert level to 5, the highest on the scale. Exclusion zone of 20 kilometres is set up and tens of thousands of people are evacuated.

12 JUNE
Exclusion zone is widened to 30 kilometres. Main eruption begins.

15 JUNE
Eruption reaches its peak with a series of giant explosions, pyroclastic flows and lahars.

EARLY JULY
Eruption gases spread right around the world.

JULY-OCTOBER
Seasonal rains set off more lahars.

MID-SEPTEMBER
Eruption finally stops.

Eruption warnings

The volcanologists had a difficult job to do. On the one hand they wanted to make sure local people were safe, but on the other they did not want to call for an expensive evacuation if the volcano was not going to become dangerous. The team worked closely with local officials, keeping them informed on the progress of the eruption and when the explosive phase was likely to happen. They also showed video recordings of pyroclastic flows and mudflows, so that people could see their dangers. In addition, they devised a system of eruption alert levels, ranging from 1 to 5.

In late May, a sharp increase in sulphur dioxide levels in the gas coming from the volcano indicated that magma was rising quickly towards the surface. By early June, earthquakes were occurring just under the summit and a lava dome was growing in the crater. The scientists knew that an explosive eruption was coming soon. They raised the alert level to 5. Tens of thousands of people were evacuated from a zone within 20 kilometres of the volcano, including the Clark Air Base.

In early June, volcanologists installed tiltmeters around the volcano to measure how the ground was rising. They showed that magma was pushing up from below.

Gigantic explosions

Pinatubo began to explode on 12 June, creating an eruption column 24,000 metres high. The exclusion zone was widened to 30 kilometres. By 13 June, a total of 58,000 people had been evacuated. Two days later the eruption reached its peak. A series of gigantic explosions continued all day. The ash fell everywhere from an eruption column 40 kilometres high. Lumps of rock the size of apples landed up to 25 kilometres from the volcano.

Pyroclastic flows formed as parts of the eruption column collapsed. They flowed up to 20 kilometres from the summit, hitting nearly all the areas indicated on the hazard maps. They deposited vast amounts of ash and rock that filled canyons hundreds of metres deep, leaving a flat, featureless landscape.

Continued effects

By coincidence, Typhoon Yunya hit the island of Luzon at the same time as the eruption. The area was deluged with rain, which mixed with the ash and formed giant lahars that swept down the volcano's slopes into the river valleys. The eruption continued until September, but became less violent. When it finally stopped, the top of Mount Pinatubo had been blown off. In its place was a caldera (crater) measuring 2 kilometres across.

Pyroclastic flows were one of the main hazards of Mount Pinatubo. The photographer who took this picture was lucky to escape the hot, billowing, fast-moving cloud of ash and gas.

ERUPTED MATERIAL

Mount Pinatubo erupted an incredible 9 cubic kilometres of ash and rock. Two-thirds of it was carried down the volcano's slopes in pyroclastic flows, and about half of that was carried away in mudflows. The other third of the material went into the atmosphere and eventually fell over a wide area.

MOUNT PINATUBO, PHILIPPINES, 1991

ERUPTION COSTS

- 900 deaths
- 200,000 people evacuated
- 100,000 square kilometres buried by mudflows during eruption
- 400,000 square kilometres affected by later flows

Ash from Mount Pinatubo darkened the sky and smothered everything on the ground with a thick, grey deposit.

Ash effects

Mount Pinatubo blew ash 25,000 metres into the atmosphere. At Clark Air Base it was dark in the middle of the day, and in Manila ash fell like brown snow. Ash fell on houses, soaked up rainwater, and the weight of the wet ash made roofs and walls collapse. An estimated 18 million tonnes of sulphur dioxide were blown into the atmosphere. It took about three weeks for the gas to spread right around the world. The sulphur dioxide reflected sunlight, and global temperatures fell by about 0.5°C. The gas also temporarily damaged the ozone layer and caused some spectacular sunsets.

Devastating mudflows

Mudflows were the most destructive element of the Mount Pinatubo eruption. The thick mud barged through and swept over many communities, and left others completely buried. In all, nearly 100 square kilometres of farmland were ruined by the mud, which smothered crops. The mud also blocked streams and rivers, causing floods. Many ponds used for fish farming were filled with ash. Hundreds of thousands of people across Luzon were left without work.

The mudflows continued for months as it was monsoon season – the rainiest time of the year – and rains washed more ash off the volcano's slopes. All the road bridges within 30 kilometres of Pinatubo were destroyed and more towns were buried or flooded. The mudflows returned with the monsoon season for many years. In the five years after the eruption, 400 square kilometres of land were affected.

During the eruption of 1991, and for years afterwards, mudflows buried whole towns and villages such as Bacolor, pictured here.

The human cost

The eruption of Mount Pinatubo killed about 900 people. Some died in pyroclastic flows, some in mudflows, some as their homes collapsed under the weight of ash and some from disease in refugee camps. More than 42,000 houses were destroyed. Overall the eruption affected a million lives. However, thousands of lives were saved by monitoring, communications between scientists and officials, education and quick thinking. The evacuation of 200,000 people was the largest ever to be made in response to volcanic hazards.

Pinatubo today

Mount Pinatubo is dormant again, but mudflows are still a threat during heavy rains. Earth embankments and dams have been built to contain the flows and trap the mud. There is now a permanent danger zone within 10 kilometres of the summit. The Pinatubo Volcano Observatory monitors the volcano with a network of instruments. Forests are beginning to regrow on the volcano's slopes, but they will take many years to return to their original thickness. Farmers are growing crops again in the new soil formed from the mudflows.

AETA PEOPLE

The Aeta are an ethnic group in the Philippines, who were the first ever inhabitants of the islands. The Pinatubo Aeta lived in settlements on the slopes of Mount Pinatubo and the volcano was sacred to them. About 20,000 Aeta people lost their homes permanently in the eruption.

SOUFRIERE HILLS, MONTSERRAT, SINCE 1995

The Soufriere Hills volcano stands on the Caribbean island of Montserrat. It has been erupting continuously since 1995. The eruption has had a major impact on this small island. Half the island has become a no-go zone, thousands of people have left and the capital has been abandoned. But life continues on Montserrat, and the eruption is monitored all the time.

The geography of Montserrat

Montserrat is one of the Lesser Antilles, a chain of islands around the edge of the Caribbean Sea. All these islands were formed by volcanic activity. They are situated above a subduction zone where the edge of the North American tectonic plate slides under the Caribbean plate. Montserrat is 16 kilometres long and 10 kilometres wide. Its hills are covered with lush green forests.

The Soufriere Hills volcano is at the southern end of the island. The volcano stands 1,000 metres high and its summit is made up of several domes of solidified lava. Before the 1995 eruption, it had been dormant for hundreds of years. Two other ranges of hills on Montserrat, the Centre Hills and the Silver Hills, are the remains of extinct volcanoes.

ISLAND POPULATION

Montserrat is an overseas colony of the UK. Its population is currently 4,700, but before the eruption it was about 12,000. The capital used to be Plymouth, but the government offices are now in Brades in the north of the island. Many people work as subsistence farmers and tourism is vital for the economy.

The Soufriere Hills volcano sent up a huge eruption column which collapsed to produce devastating pyroclastic flows.

Soufriere erupts

Some earthquake activity in 1992 showed that Soufriere was coming to life, but the eruption did not begin until 18 July 1995, when the volcano started throwing out steam and ash. In August, a small eruption caused darkness in the city of Plymouth for 15 minutes and left the streets blanketed in ash. Then in September a lava dome began growing in the volcano's crater, and October saw the first mudflows sweep down from the summit. In 1996, the lava dome grew and collapsed twice, causing pyroclastic flows. That September an explosion of magma created an eruption column 25,000 metres high, which left deep ash across the south of the island. The next year there was a series of explosions, and major pyroclastic flows reached Plymouth and other towns.

LONG BUT LESS STRONG

The eruptions of the Soufriere Hills volcano have been quite small compared to those at Mount Pinatubo or Mount St Helens, but they have lasted far longer and continue today.

SOUFRIERE HILLS, MONTSERRAT, SINCE 1995

Evacuations

The authorities on Montserrat ordered the first evacuations from the southern end of the island in August 1995, a few weeks after the eruption began. Thousands of people were moved to the safe area at the northern end of the island. Some were given temporary accommodation in schools, churches and community centres. Others moved in with relatives and friends, or rented houses. They were given food by the government.

This is all that is left of Plymouth, the capital of Montserrat, which was buried by ash from the pyroclastic flows.

Abandonment

Many people moved home again as the volcano settled down, but fresh eruptions in 1996 made the south of the island too dangerous. Plymouth was abandoned in 1996 and left to be buried by ash. Public services, such as the local hospital and telephone company, had to be relocated. Shopkeepers from Plymouth reopened their businesses in other villages or on roadsides. The government built houses for people who were in temporary accommodation, and some people moved their homes to the north by truck.

EYEWITNESS

❝ We won't give up so easy. We'll carry on till we can come back to Plymouth. ❞

Nigel Osborne, who ran a supermarket in Plymouth but has now set it up in another town

Eruption effects

The landscape around the Soufriere Hills was transformed into an ash-covered wasteland. Trees and other plants were killed. Plymouth gradually became almost completely buried. By the end of 1997, many buildings had virtually vanished. The airport had been destroyed and the docks at Plymouth had become too dangerous to use. The whole southern end of the island was uninhabitable. Thousands of homes and other buildings were ruined. The pyroclastic flows of 1997 killed 19 people. Most of these fatalities were people who had stayed in the danger area despite the evacuation.

The eruption and evacuations in the Soufriere Hills destroyed Montserrat's tourism industry. Hotels and restaurants closed because of lack of business, and passing cruise ships no longer stopped. The closures left one in two people out of work.

MOVING AWAY

Montserrat is a small island and there was not enough space in the north for all the evacuees. Some stayed, but two-thirds of the islanders decided to leave Montserrat. They went to other Caribbean islands and to the UK. In 1998, the people of Montserrat were granted the right to live in the UK permanently if they did not want to go home. Many still hope to return to Montserrat one day if the eruptions stop.

Volcanic ash is made up of very small particles. It drifts in the air and settles on every surface, and is very difficult to clear away.

SOUFRIERE HILLS, MONTSERRAT, SINCE 1995

Continuing eruptions

The Soufriere Hills volcano is still erupting and there is no sign that this is coming to an end. There are regular outbursts of steam and ash. A number of lava domes have grown and then collapsed, setting off debris avalanches and pyroclastic flows. There are regular mudflows during heavy rains, which are frequent on Montserrat. Although the eruption is not as violent now as it was in 1995-7, the pyroclastic flows and mudflows mean that the south of the island is still dangerous for people to return to.

Montserrat today

Today, Montserrat is still divided into a safe zone in the north of the island and an unsafe zone in the south. The unsafe zone covers about two-thirds of the island around the volcano. It contains the old capital Plymouth, which remains abandoned. People are not allowed to enter the unsafe zone without permission. The safe zone is not threatened by the continuing eruption, although it sometimes gets dusted with volcanic ash.

New government offices have been built in the north, together with new docks and a new airport, which was opened in 2005. The UK government gave money to help with these projects. The new airport is a boost for the tourism industry, which is thriving again. The Montserrat tourist board advertises the volcano as a visitor attraction. It provides an opportunity to see an active volcano and its effects at close range. There are purpose-built viewing areas for tourists. Some of these are in a section of the unsafe zone that is opened during the day for visitors. Tourists can also get good views of Plymouth and its covering of ash.

HURRICANE HUGO

The eruption of the Soufriere Hills volcano was the second natural disaster to affect Montserrat in the space of six years. In 1989, the island was hit full-on by Hurricane Hugo which damaged more than 90 per cent of the buildings. The island had almost recovered when the volcano came to life.

A tourist yacht cruises towards Montserrat. Thousands of people now visit the island to get a close-up view of an active volcano.

The Montserrat Volcano Observatory

The Montserrat Volcano Observatory was set up in 1995, soon after the eruption began. At the time it was operated by an international team of volcanologists from the West Indies, the UK and the USA. Its job was to monitor the volcano and provide information on its dangers to the authorities. In 2003, the observatory was relocated to a new building 6 kilometres from the volcano, just outside the unsafe zone. Volcanologists from the observatory continue to monitor the volcano and keep the island's inhabitants aware of the current dangers. They also educate the public and tourists about the volcano and the science of volcanology.

ERUPTION COSTS

- 19 deaths
- Plymouth destroyed
- South of island abandoned
- Docks and airport destroyed
- Two-thirds of population left Montserrat

NYIRAGONGO, DEMOCRATIC REPUBLIC OF CONGO, 2002

Nyiragongo, in the Democratic Republic of Congo (DRC), is one of Africa's most active volcanoes. It has been active almost non-stop for many decades. In 2002, lava from Nyiragongo flowed through the streets of the city of Goma, destroying many buildings. There was no warning. Hundreds of thousands of people fled from the city and needed urgent help, which came from international aid agencies.

Geography of Nyiragongo

Nyiragongo is in the Rift Valley in eastern Africa, the site of a divergent boundary between two tectonic plates. There are several more volcanoes in a chain along the north-south line of this boundary. Nyiragongo is a stratovolcano but it does not erupt explosively like most stratovolcanoes. At the summit is a crater about 800 metres deep and in the bottom of the crater is a lake of red-hot lava. Nyiragongo is one of only a few volcanoes in the world that have a permanent crater lake. During periods of high activity the level of the lake rises as fresh lava flows in from below.

The eruption

On 17 January 2002, lava began flowing from wide splits (called fissures) that opened up on the slopes of Nyiragongo. The lava flowed south down the slopes, draining from the lake in the crater. The largest flow to hit Goma came from a vent just 4 kilometres north of the city. This flow entered Lake Kivu and formed new land as it cooled. Lava flowed from the volcano for about 24 hours.

LAVA LAKES

A lava lake forms where molten magma rises very high inside a volcano, flooding the crater. Lava lakes usually have a shiny grey crust on top because the atmosphere constantly cools the surface, making it become partially solid. The crust is rarely more than a few minutes or hours old as it keeps moving in a cycle, breaking up and sinking down into the molten lava below.

Lava flows from gaping cracks in the ground on the slopes of Nyiragongo.

Goma cut in half

Two lava flows hit Goma. The largest travelled over the airport runway, caused the aviation fuel store to explode, and then poured through the eastern side of the city and into the adjoining lake. It knocked down some buildings and buried others, leaving a swathe of black rock. A smaller lava flow came to a stop in the west of the city. About one-sixth of the city's area was engulfed. The power station was hit, and people were left with no electricity or running water.

UNSETTLED TERRITORY

Nyiragongo is close to the border between the Democratic Republic of Congo (formerly Zaire) and Rwanda. Goma is 18 kilometres to the south, on the shores of Lake Kivu. At the start of 2002, the political situation in the DRC was unstable and Goma was controlled by rebel forces and Rwandan soldiers.

ERUPTION COSTS

- **More than 100 deaths**
- **One-sixth of Goma destroyed by lava**
- **Power station destroyed**
- **300,000 people evacuated from Goma**
- **60,000 people made homeless**

A mass evacuation

The lava flows came as a surprise to the residents of Goma. As the flows approached, hundreds of thousands of people fled from the city. Between 200,000 and 300,000 evacuees crossed the border to the city of Gisenyi in Rwanda, where they spent the night sleeping on the streets. People also fled to the west, but many stayed in Goma to protect their homes from looters (thieves). Over the next few days, most people returned to Goma. More than 100 people died in the lava flows, in collapsing buildings and in an explosion at a petrol station. Many were burned as they crossed the red-hot rock. About 60,000 people lost their homes to the lava and fires.

International help

The Democratic Republic of Congo is a very poor country and was unable to help the victims of Nyiragongo. Luckily there were several international aid agencies in the area, helping refugees from a previous civil war in Rwanda. They included the United Nations World Food Programme, Oxfam and Médecins Sans Frontières. Together with the government of Rwanda, they set up camps for displaced people in Rwanda and supplied tents, blankets and food to them and the people in Goma. Disease was a serious risk, as people were drinking from Lake Kivu, so setting up supplies of clean drinking water and sanitation systems was a priority.

A child salvages building materials from the jumbled, solidified remains of the lava flows that cut through Goma.

Women prepare water at one of the aid camps in Goma, set up by international organizations for people displaced by the eruption of Nyiragongo.

Goma Volcano Observatory

The Goma Volcano Observatory (GVO) existed before the 2002 eruption but was poorly funded and had little equipment. Its staff warned that an eruption of Nyiragongo was likely, but their concern was ignored. An international team arrived within days of the eruption, and the GVO now has more support and a new network of instruments. It is responsible for monitoring Nyiragongo and other volcanoes in the area.

Nyiragongo and Goma today

New buildings have sprung up in place of some of Goma's lava flows. The recovery has been helped by an improvement in the political situation. Nyiragongo is still active, and its crater contains a fresh lava lake. Lava flows are not the only risk to local people. Nyiragongo's eruptions give out as much sulphur dioxide as all the other volcanoes in the world combined. The gas causes acid rain in the area, which damages crops and pollutes drinking water.

EYEWITNESS

❝ Everything is destroyed. We're staying on here to guard what's left against looters. But of course we have no guests, and the fumes from the lava are very strong and unpleasant. ❞

Omar Suleiman, manager of the Lumamba Hotel in Goma where lava buried the whole of the ground floor and set light to much of the building and its contents

Eruption prediction and protection

Volcanologists work hard trying to understand why volcanoes erupt, studying what happens during eruptions and attempting to predict when volcanoes are going to come to life. They use several techniques and many technical instruments to monitor volcanoes.

Quakes and bulges

A volcanologist's most important weapon is seismology, which is the study of earthquakes. Small earthquakes show that magma is moving underground, and eruptions are always preceded by hundreds of them. Earthquakes can be detected by instruments called seismometers. Volcanologists normally place several of these around a volcano, which allows them to pinpoint where earthquakes come from. Volcanologists also monitor ground movements. If the ground bulges, it means that magma is pushing up from below. Ground movements are measured using tiltmeters, and by checking the position of markers on the ground using lasers and the global positioning system (GPS).

Heat and gas

Measuring temperature is another way of gauging volcanic activity. The temperature of the ground rises as magma approaches the surface. Volcanologists measure temperature with electronic thermometers and infra-red sensors. They also take samples of gases coming from a volcano's vents. A high level of sulphur dioxide indicates that fresh magma is moving towards the surface.

A scientist from the US Geological Survey uses an electronic distance-measuring device to measure the dome of the South Sister volcano, USA.

Building a picture

Remote sensing is another useful tool for volcanologists. From space, satellites can build up surface-temperature maps, photograph how clouds of ash and gas are spreading and use radar to make three-dimensional maps of volcanoes. Volcanologists can also get an idea of what the effects of an eruption might be by studying the deposits of ash and other debris from previous eruptions. These old deposits tell them how far mudflows and pyroclastic flows have reached in the past, and which areas are therefore most at risk in the future.

Protecting the public

Careful disaster planning is as important as accurate prediction. Local officials, the emergency services and the general public all need to know what action to take if volcanologists recommend an evacuation. In some places where cities are threatened by mudflows and pyroclastic flows, barriers and channels have been built to divert the flows. For example, the Indonesian city of Yogyakarta is protected from lahars from the volcano Merapi by a series of mud-capturing dams called *sabo* dams.

Increasing success

The case studies in this book show that volcanologists are getting better at predicting eruptions. Mount Pelée killed so many people because nobody understood pyroclastic flows in 1902. The eruption of Mount St Helens was predicted, but its sideways blast taught volcanologists that volcanoes can erupt in unexpected ways. The lahar from Nevado del Ruiz was also predicted, but people died there because of poor planning. There were successes at Pinatubo in 1991 and in Montserrat in 1995, where early warnings led people to be evacuated safely. Perhaps in the future more disasters will be successfully avoided.

A volcanologist collects a sample of lava for examination. His clothes protect him from the heat of the lava flow.

Glossary

atmosphere The layer of air surrounding Earth.

caldera A very large crater (more than a kilometre across) left when the top of a volcano sinks after an explosive eruption.

civil war A war fought between groups of people from the same country.

colony A country, or region within a country, that is ruled by another country.

convergent boundary A line where the edges of two tectonic plates are moving towards each other (or converging).

debris Scattered material, such as tree branches or building rubble, that has been dislodged or broken and left behind after a volcanic eruption or other disaster.

divergent boundary A line where two tectonic plates are moving away from each other (or diverging).

earthquake Shaking of the ground caused by underground movement of rocks.

eruption When gas and ash, lava or solid pieces of rock blast from a volcano.

evacuate To move away from a dangerous place to somewhere safe.

exclusion zone An area that the public are not allowed to go into.

GPS Global positioning system, allowing accurate location of points on Earth using sensors on satellites in space.

hazard map A map showing which areas are at risk from lava or pyroclastic flows, lahars or ash fall during an eruption.

lahar A landslide of volcanic ash mixed with water, forming mud.

lava The name given to magma when it comes out of a volcano.

magma Hot, molten underground rock.

monsoon A seasonal wind that blows across Asia, bringing heavy rains.

observatory A place from which scientists watch and study a volcano.

ozone layer A layer of the atmosphere, containing a gas called ozone, that protects Earth from harmful rays from the Sun by absorbing much of their energy.

pyroclast A piece of rock (solid or molten) that is ejected from a volcano, such as an ash particle, a cinder or a piece of lava.

pyroclastic flow A cloud made up of very hot gas, ash and rock that flows down the side of a volcano like an avalanche.

sanitation The collection and treatment of waste water.

seismometer An instrument that detects earthquakes and measures their strength.

subduction zone Where the edge of one tectonic plate slides beneath another.

sulphur dioxide A polluting gas that is often given out by a volcanic eruption.

summit The very top of a hill, mountain or volcano.

tectonic plates Giant sections of the Earth's crust that move slowly in relation to each other, giving rise to earthquakes, volcanoes and other natural hazards.

tiltmeter An instrument that measures the slope of the ground, allowing scientists to detect when the ground bulges or sinks.

tsunami A series of waves at sea, caused by an undersea earthquake, landslide or volcanic explosion.

typhoon A hurricane (storm) that occurs around the Pacific and Indian Oceans.

vent A hole in a volcano (at the top or in the sides) that lava, ash or gas erupt from.

volcanologist A scientist who studies volcanoes.

Further Information

Books

Nature's Fury: Volcano!
Anita Ganeri
Franklin Watts, 2006

Earth's Changing Landscape: Earthquakes and Volcanoes
Chris Oxlade
Franklin Watts, 2004

Teach Yourself Volcanoes
David A. Rothery
Teach Yourself Books, 2003

Natural Disasters (Eyewitness Guides)
Claire Watts
Dorling Kindersley, 2006

Websites

http://vulcan.wr.usgs.gov/Volcanoes
Links to information on hundreds of volcanoes, including all those in this book.

http://www.volcano.si.edu
Home page of the Global Volcanism Program. Information on every active volcano around the world.

http://www.mvo.ms
Website of the Montserrat Volcano Observatory.

http://faculty.gg.uwyo.edu/heller/SedMovs /Pyroclastic.htm Video of pyroclastic flows from Montserrat.